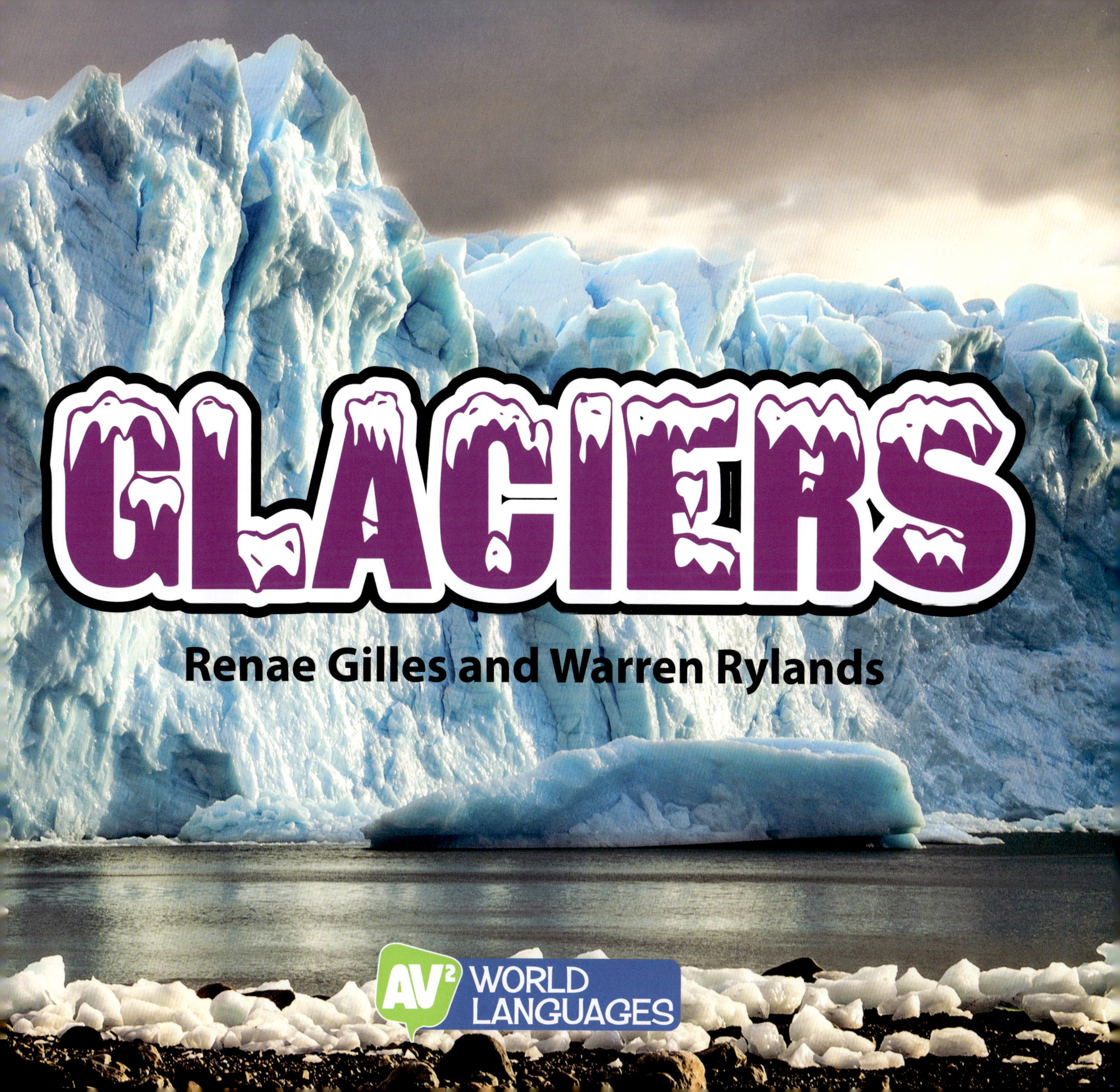

GLACIERS

Renae Gilles and Warren Rylands

AV² WORLD LANGUAGES

AV2 WORLD LANGUAGES

Go to **openlightbox.com**, and enter the book's unique code.

BOOK CODE

AVN53568

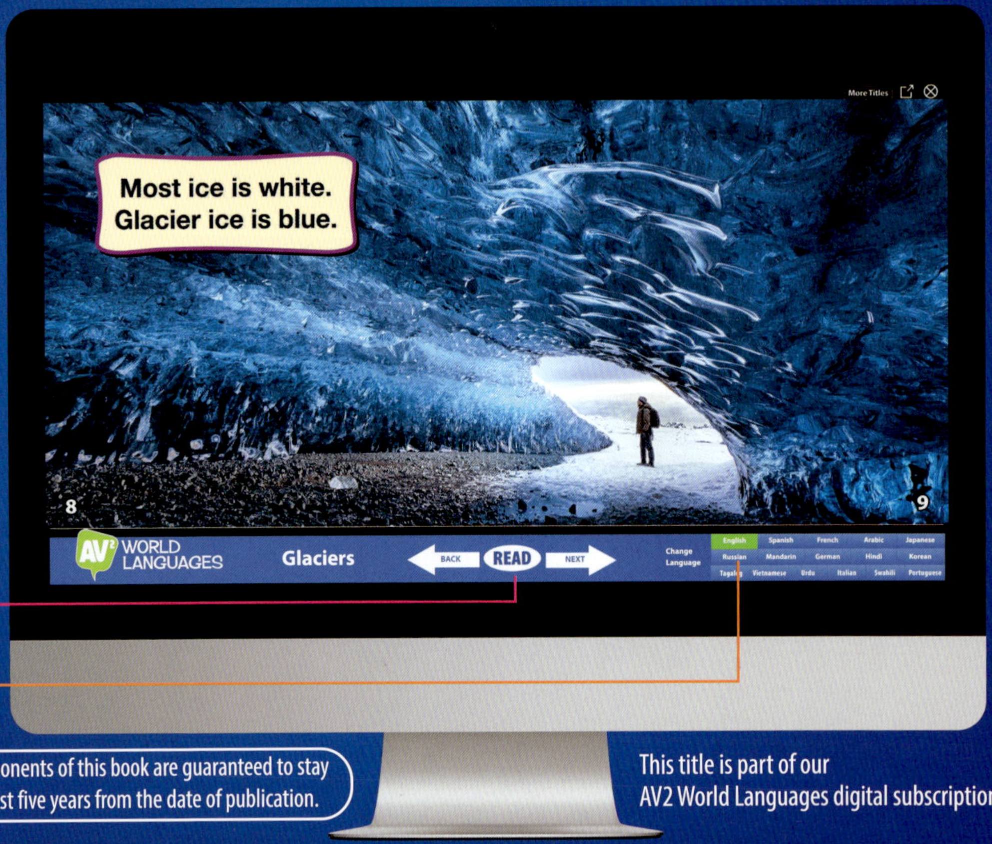

Easily move through highly visual pages.

Toggle between your **16 books** in **16 languages.**

The digital components of this book are guaranteed to stay active for at least five years from the date of publication.

This title is part of our AV2 World Languages digital subscription.

Published by Lightbox Learning Inc.
276 5th Avenue, Suite 704 #917
New York, NY 10001
Website: www.openlightbox.com

Library of Congress Control Number: 2023933526

ISBN 978-1-7911-5557-5 (hardcover)
ISBN 978-1-7911-5558-2 (multi-user eBook)

Printed in Guangzhou, China
1 2 3 4 5 6 7 8 9 0 27 26 25 24 23

042023
102322

Project Coordinator: John Willis
Designer: Mandy Christiansen

Every reasonable effort has been made to trace ownership and to obtain permission to reprint copyright material. The publisher would be pleased to have any errors or omissions brought to its attention so that they may be corrected in subsequent printings.

The publisher acknowledges Alamy, Getty Images, and Shutterstock as the primary image suppliers for this title.

Access all of the AV2 World Languages titles with our digital subscription.

1-Year World Languages Subscription ISBN
978-1-4896-8345-8

Sign up for a **FREE SUBSCRIPTION**
openlightbox.com/trial

Glaciers

In this book, you will learn about

- how they look
- where they are
- what they do

and much more!

A glacier is a large chunk of ice.

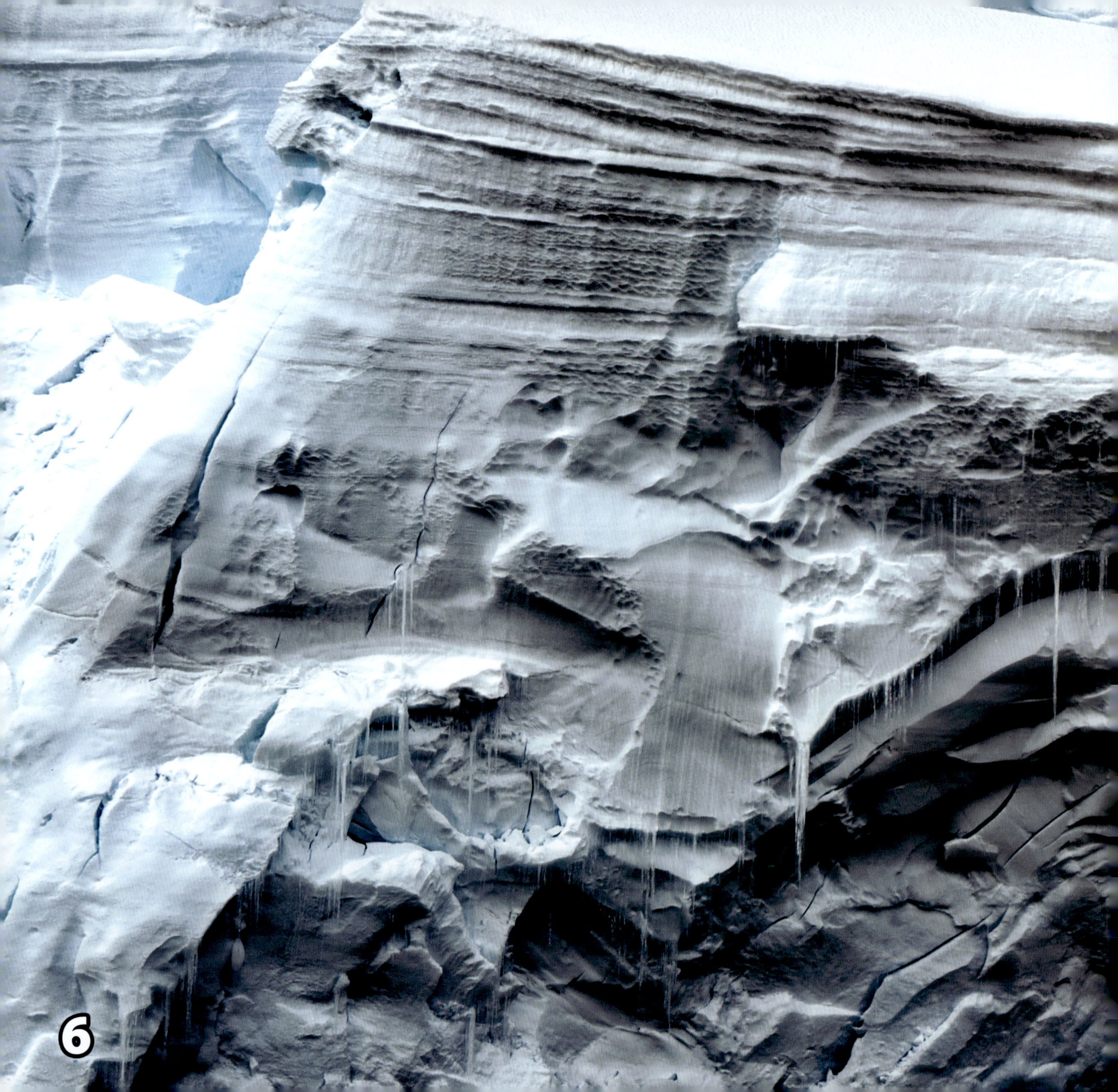
6

Glaciers are made of snow that has piled up for hundreds of years.

Most ice is white.
Glacier ice is blue.

Most of the world's fresh water is in glaciers.

Glaciers are in places where it stays cold all year.

Glaciers can be on mountains. There are glaciers on Mount Kilimanjaro in Africa.

Glaciers melt slowly. They move by sliding on top of the melting water.

18

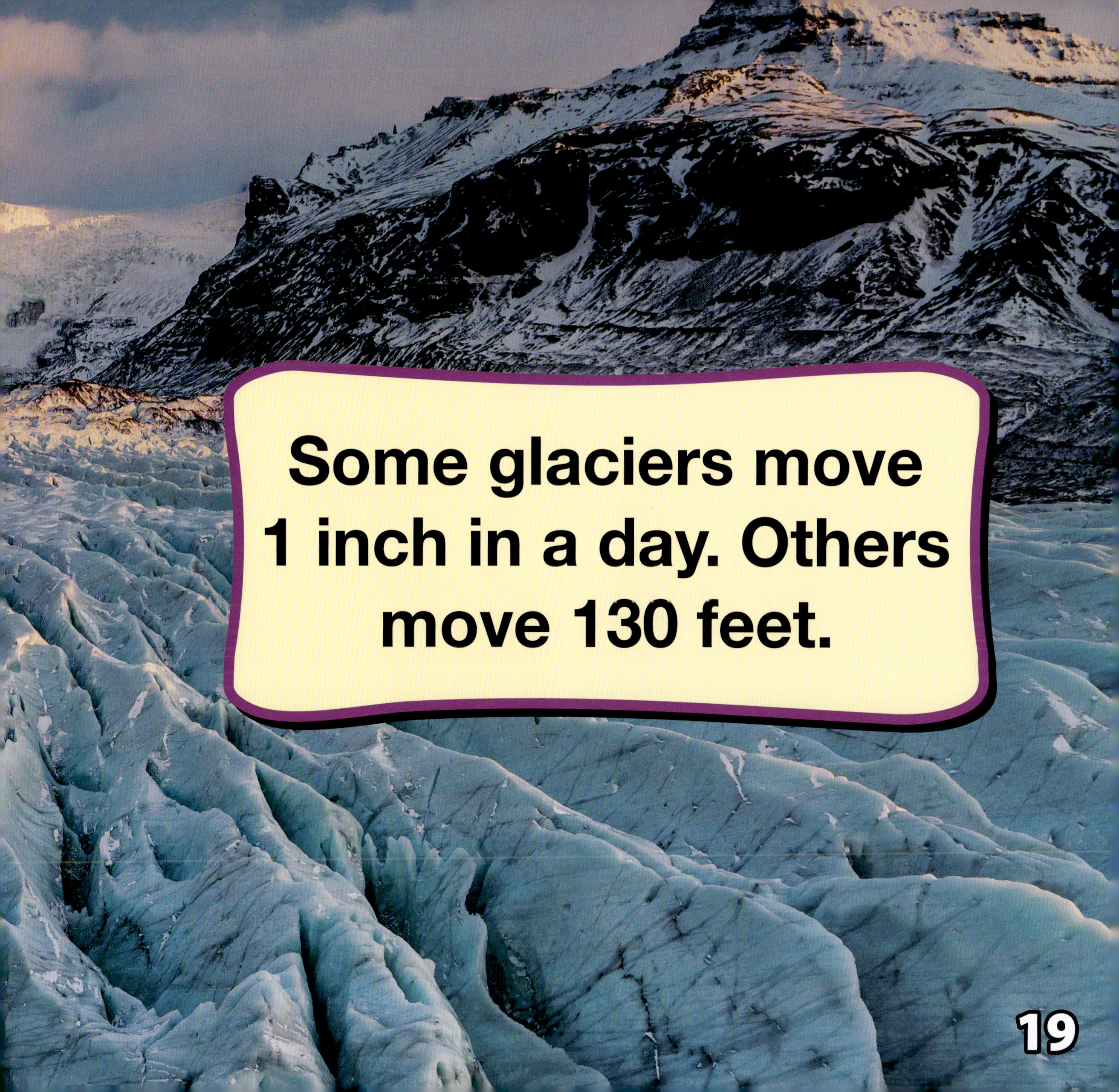

Some glaciers move 1 inch in a day. Others move 130 feet.

Glaciers are an important part of Earth. They must be protected.

GLACIERS BY THE NUMBERS

Oceans would be **200 feet deeper** if all glaciers melted.

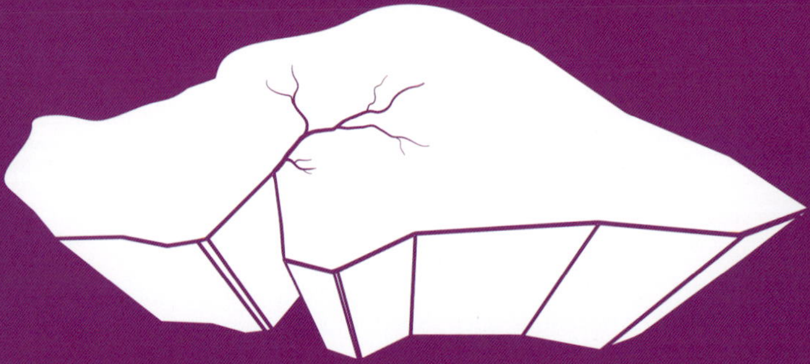

The **biggest** glacier is the **Lambert Glacier** in Antarctica.

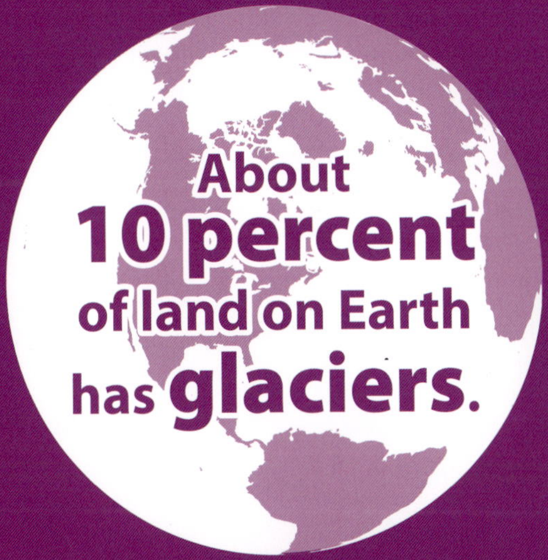

About **10 percent** of land on Earth has **glaciers.**

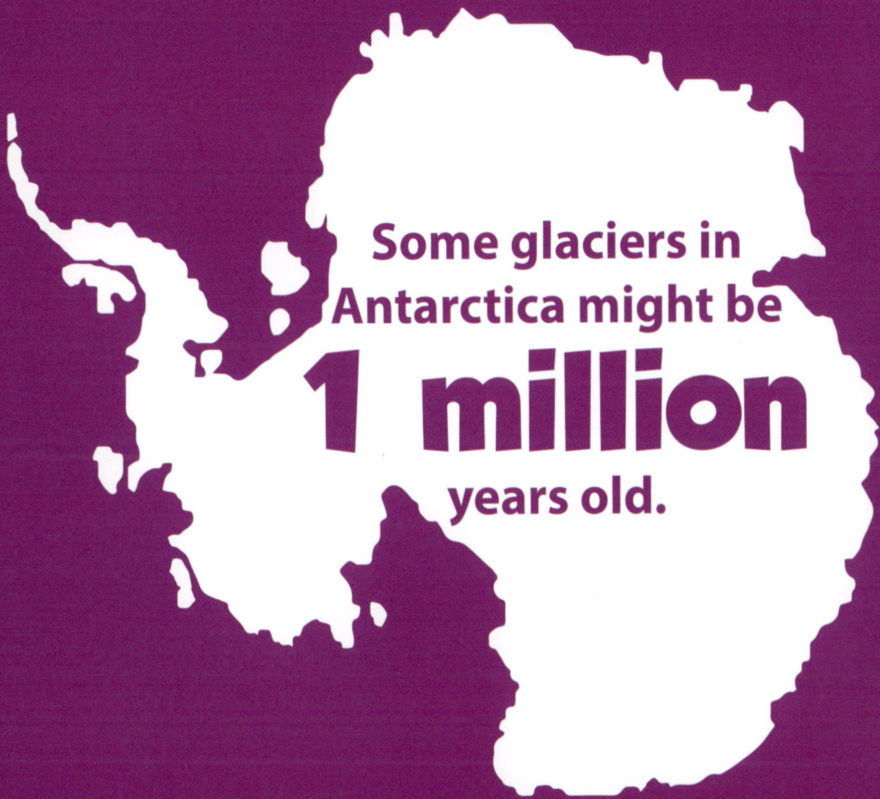

Some glaciers in Antarctica might be **1 million** years old.

Glaciers are in **47 countries.**

KEY WORDS

Research has shown that as much as 65 percent of all written material published in English is made up of 300 words. These 300 words cannot be taught using pictures or learned by sounding them out. They must be recognized by sight. This book contains 38 common sight words to help young readers improve their reading fluency and comprehension. This book also teaches young readers several important content words, such as proper nouns. These words are paired with pictures to aid in learning and improve understanding.

Page	Sight Words First Appearance
4	a, is, large, of
7	are, for, has, made, that, up, years
8	most, white
11	in, the, water, world
12	all, it, places, where
14	be, can, mountains, on, there
16	by, move, they
19	day, feet, others, some
20	an, Earth, important, must, part

Page	Content Words First Appearance
4	chunk, glacier, ice
7	hundreds, snow
8	blue
14	Africa, Mount Kilimanjaro
19	inch